I0500796

BY THE SAME AUTHOR

The Rise and Fall of Occupy Wall Street

The Party's Over: Communist Organization in the Modern World

On the Collapse of American Capitalism

Their Socialism and Ours

R. Shay

WHOCANAFFORDA PRESS

2013 by R. Shay

Paperback first published in 2013 by Whocanafforda Press.

All rights reserved.

Set in Times New Roman

ISBN-10: 1482582600
ISBN-13: 9781482582604

Contents

Introduction 7

An answer in the form of a question 9

Proletarian revolutions 15

Petty-bourgeois revolutions 29

National-democratic revolutions 59

Conclusion 63

Notes 25

Time line 71

Introduction

"Socialism has been a failure everywhere that it has been attempted." Such is the refrain heard time and time again whenever even a hint of the word socialism emerges. The statement has been repeated so often that today it appears as an unchallengeable truism.

As global capitalism continues to descend into its worst crisis since the Great Depression, thus intensifying the pain and suffering it inherently inflicts, millions are opening their eyes and searching out alternatives. There is a clear, international reawakening. Socialism is now being investigated by the largest number of people since the destruction of the USSR took place two decades ago.

This situation has lead to a reopening of the historical tomes so recently proclaimed to be forever closed. "Historical verdicts" are being reconsidered and even swept away completely. A new generation is searching for a way out of the enveloping darkness imposed upon it by a failing system.

These conditions have presented an opening for the emergence of this work, which intends to help demystify both the past and the present in order to better arm those who are destined to create the future.

A comprehensive examination of these issues is certainly necessary. If this humble attempt does not draw all the correct conclusions, it is my hope that it at least encourages the reader to make the right inquiries.

An answer in the form of a question

In order to move forward in this effort, it is first necessary to look back. Many of the questions of the day can best be answered through an investigation of days gone by.

Has socialism proved itself unworkable with repeated failure? We can only arrive at a satisfactory reply to this question by first defining socialism, or, more precisely, the various *socialisms*, and examining attempts to put them into practice.

Though the underlying ideas trace their roots to a far more distant past, the French aristocrat Henri de Saint-Simon is often credited with coining the term "socialism" in the first half 19th Century. Whether or not this is entirely accurate is not of any real importance for our purposes. What is certain is that Saint-Simon, Robert Owen, Charles Fourier, et al., all belonged to the school of utopian socialism.

Limited as they were by their class origins and the circumstances in which they lived, these reformers sought to ease the social antagonisms created by the rise of capitalism by means of well-designed plans, which they believed could be peacefully enacted. They were well aware of the struggle between the capitalist and working classes—indeed their ideas arose as a direct result of this struggle—but they had only become acquainted with it in its infancy. Consequently, they failed to see any potential of change resulting from this clash of class interests. Instead, they offered up intricate plans—which they viewed as blueprints for the best possible societies—direct to the capitalist rulers, convinced that those in power would not be able to reject their well thought out schemes. In the end, this trend was eliminated in the main by the forward thrust of history itself. All that remained in the form positive contributions were to be found in the extensive criticisms of capitalist society offered up. Few utopian socialists exist today.

Those few that can still be found are most often recently awoken, and will move on once they deepen their understanding, or individual radicals looking for a way to "escape" capitalism.

The modern equivalent of utopian socialism can be found in bourgeois (or capitalist) socialism. Reflecting the interests of a class already in power, bourgeois socialism seeks only to perfect the existing system. The bourgeois socialists wish to eliminate, or lessen, the negative effects of the capitalist system (war, unemployment, homelessness, etc.) with generally socialistic measures, while at the same time preserving the capitalist mode of production. In other words, they want all the advantages of capitalism with none of the social ills that come along with it. They want to maintain class divisions but eliminate class struggle. This is the socialism practiced by the majority of the "official" Social Democratic, Democratic Socialist, Socialist, Communist and Labor parties today. Whenever the capitalist ruling class finds itself in danger of being overthrown by the working class, it often relies on capitalist socialism to bring the workers "under control" with a combination of rhetoric and treachery. This was the case with the Social Democrats in Germany in 1919, the Communist Party of France in 1968, etc. Today, most of the "official" parties of bourgeois socialism are not even able to offer preservation of past reforms. Instead, they join the ruling block in its campaign of austerity.

Little mention is needed of feudal socialism, which disappeared long ago. The aristocrats who belonged to this camp attacked the ills of the capitalist society that ruined them, but did so only in an attempt to convince the working class to fight for a return to feudalism. Unable to run the film of history in reverse, the feudal socialists ended in miserable failure. The only remnants of this trend are today found in its offshoot: clerical socialism.

The clerical socialists carefully select quotes from the

11

holy books of their religion of choice to show that their patron saints were the "original" opponents of injustice, greed, etc. They see "sin" as the sole cause of all problems and thus can only offer the "alternative" of submission, sacrifice, martyrdom, etc. This little school is constantly diminishing, though it may be resurrected here and there in times of crisis by witchdoctors and soothsayers who seek to derail struggles, take the reigns of power, or both.

By far the most prominent form of socialism, at least in the last eight decades, has been petty-bourgeois socialism. This school of socialism originated as an expression of the interests of the petty-bourgeoisie, a class shaped by the rise of capitalism. The traditional members of this class (i.e. independent producers and shopkeepers), are continually disappearing as a result of their inability to compete with the much larger and more modern enterprises of the capitalists. Those who ascended from the working class are most often driven back into it, as their attempts to "get ahead" crash miserably against the hard rocks of capitalist reality. A certain layer of the petty-bourgeoisie is maintained to fill the "gaps" left in the industrialized economy. They provide some of the products and services that "big capitalism" either cannot or will not. Another layer of the established petty-bourgeoisie have found their place in modern capitalism as stewards of the capitalists' apparatuses (i.e. managers, consultants, brokers, bureaucrats, police, private security and the like). The petty-bourgeoisie is accustomed to giving orders and being in control, and petty-bourgeois socialism reflects that.

The petty-bourgeois socialists view the working class as being too unskilled, uneducated and unfamiliar with decision making to rule directly. Therefore, they contend, socialism requires the rule of an enlightened group: none other than themselves.

But as is often the case, the petty-bourgeois socialists who see themselves as future rulers do not publicly promote

12

their class interests. In order to win the allegiance of working people, in order to retain a group of toilers to control, petty-bourgeois socialism does not openly proclaim itself an instrument of the petty-bourgeoisie. Instead, it blankets itself with the traditional red flag of the workers' movement and adopts a number of its slogans, all the while replacing any mention of class with vague calls to "the people" or "the masses."

During periods of relative class peace, when capitalism is in no immediate danger of being overthrown, this school of socialism usually enjoys little support. All types of socialist and communist groups may abound, headed up of course by aspirant petty-bourgeois leaders claiming to represent the One True Socialism, but they are largely ignored by the class a whole, largely content with its position.

It is when the very existence of the petty-bourgeois as a class becomes endangered by proletarian revolution that petty-bourgeois socialism most often surges in popularity.

Faced with extinction, the petty-bourgeoisie sees no other alternative than to attempt to rule directly, and thus takes power. This is exactly what occurred in the majority of the so-called communist countries that arose in the twentieth-century.

Despite all attempts by the ruling classes to bury it forever, one last school of socialism remains: workers' (or proletarian) socialism. Workers' socialism represents the interests of the working class (i.e. the vast majority; those who neither own nor control any of the tools or technology used to make the things people need and want and are thus forced to work for those who do: the capitalists). The working class creates and distributes everything but only receives enough in return to keep itself alive and functioning in modern society – with huge sections being denied even that. The surplus created by the working class is kept by the capitalists, with a portion of the leftovers given to the petty-bourgeoisie administrators as payment for their services.

13

As society's producers, and thus the only source of wealth other than nature itself, the working class neither requires nor is able to carry out the exploitation of any other class. Because of this, the working class is the only class capable of both overthrowing capitalism and creating a classless society. By removing the obstacles to its own emancipation, the working class liberates all of humanity. The accomplishment of these tasks is not just a "good idea" but a necessity—a requirement for the working class to both to emancipate itself and to bring to an end the spiraling decent into barbarism and destruction we as humans find ourselves in today.

In practice, the institution of workers' socialism requires that the working class take control of the means of production (i.e. the tools and technology used to make the things people need and want). By abolishing the private ownership of the means of production and the specialized roles of managers, advisers, government bureaucrats and the like, thus requiring each person (other than those rendered unable by age or infirmity) to contribute to the work required to satisfy human wants and needs, the working class simultaneously abolishes wage labor, capital, and classes.

Workers' socialism then is not a specific economic system but simply the first step toward a higher form of society which will be fully realized by a new generation reared under new conditions—free from the marks of exploitation, oppression and inequality left by capitalism—with the means of satisfying the requirements of humanity as a whole.

One class can only take the place of another, ruling class by overthrowing it. That, in essence, is social revolution. In order to best analyze the various attempts made at establishing socialism throughout history, each should be viewed according to which class reigned.

There is no need to examine any of the numerous instances of bourgeois socialists at the helm of capitalist states over the years. Suffice it to say that bourgeois socialism has succeeded (for the class it serves) by helping to preserve the capitalist system.

Proletarian revolutions

Paris

The working class first attempted to take power in Paris, France, in 1871, after the defeat of Napoleon III in the Franco-Prussian war.

As a result of substantial military losses, the French government was forced to sign a peace treaty. The terms of that treaty included the ceremonial occupation of Paris by the German military. But when the German soldiers arrived in Paris, they found themselves restricted to a few small parks by the National Guard, a citizen's militia made up largely of workers, which had originally been formed to defend the city.

After having first received authorization from Germany, the new French government, led by Louis Thiers, sent its army into Paris to prevent the working class there from arming itself and attacking the Germany soldiers.

The workers of Paris refused to hand over their weapons, which included several canons that they viewed as public property. In turn, Thiers's "Government of National Defense" declared war on the city of Paris.

The National Guard arranged elections to form a governing council that would come to be known as the Paris Commune. Delegates, who received the same pay as the average worker and were subject to immediate recall at any time, were directly elected by the residents of Paris. Some of these representatives came from countries other than France. This was completely acceptable for the Commune, which had replaced the national tricolor flag with the blood-red "flag of the World Republic."

The Commune abolished the standing army in favor of the National Guard militia, which was to be made up of all persons capable of bearing arms, and decreed the separation of church and state, the transformation of all church property into national property, the removal of prayer and all religious symbols from schools, the elimination of night work in the bakeries, the suspension of all rent paid on housing, the extension of pensions to all unmarried partners and children of National Guard members, the closing of all pawnshops and the return of all of the tools of working people in their possession, the suspension of payments on all commercial debts and the elimination of interest on said debts, and the right of workers to take over any enterprise abandoned by its owner.

In relation to the latter decree, the Commune began gathering statistics on the number of factories which had been closed down by their owners and began working out plans for organization of the workers who labored within them so that the plants could be effectively reopened.

In the name of internationalism, the Vendôme Column—a monument celebrating the victories of French leader Napoleon I—was pulled down.

Working people also began organizing themselves to replace the specialists that had fled the city. All around Paris orphanages were established; private Catholic schools were secularized; and school children were provided with free food, clothing, and supplies.

The Commune "was essentially a working-class government, the produce of the struggle of the producing class against the appropriating class, the political form at last discovered under which to work out the economic emancipation of labor."[1]

But before the new revolutionary society could really get off the ground it came under attack. Less than three months after the working class had taken power, the city of Paris was assailed by the strongest army the French government could put together.

The workers' heroic attempt at defending the city proved

to be insufficient. The French army retook the city in a matter of days, gunning down 30,000 unarmed people in the streets in the process. In addition to that mass murder, the French army arrested 38,000 others and sent an additional 7,000 into permanent exile.

The working class had reached for power and saw its attempt drowned in blood. It wouldn't be the last time for either.

St. Louis

The second attempt by the working class to take power came in St. Louis, United States, in 1877.

Following a major economic collapse of the kind endemic to capitalism, the capitalists set about drastically cutting workers' wages and hours. In many cases, workers were forced to labor without pay. By 1877, they'd had enough.

What started as a railroad workers' strike in Martinsburg, West Virginia, soon spread throughout the country. Almost everywhere they went out on strike, workers were attacked. The bloodiest scenes took place in Pittsburgh, Reading and Chicago. Blood was also spilled in Philadelphia and Cumberland.

In East St. Louis, the railroad strike turned into a general strike around demands for an eight-hour working day and an end to child labor. Soon, it became much more.

Workers gathered around.

A speaker at the strike stood up and declared, "All you have to do, gentlemen, for you have the numbers, is to unite on one idea - that workingmen shall rule the country. What man makes, belongs to him, and the workingmen made this country."[2]

A black speaker sent by the levee and steamboat workers asked the strikers if they would stand behind him and his fellow

18

workers, regardless of skin color. The crowd responded with a resounding shout of "We will!"[3]

Representatives of the workers at nearly every railroad met and set about establishing the St. Louis Commune. Their first move was to halt all rail traffic other than passenger and mail trains. They took measures to protect the railroads from destruction and began to restart selected production by allowing one packing house to process 150 cows in exchange for 500 cans of beef for the city's workers.

Just as the St. Louis Commune began to pick up momentum, proving itself legitimate and gaining the support of the workers of all industries in the city, it was destroyed by force. Less than a week after the Commune had been formed, East St. Louis was attacked by 3,000 soldiers and 5,000 special police. At least 18 workers were killed, dozens were imprisoned and the Commune's organizational center was taken, marking an end to the St. Louis Commune.

Bavaria

In 1919, the working class took power for a short time in Bavaria, the largest state in Germany.

On February 19, 1919, a young aristocrat assassinated Kurt Eisner, a bourgeois socialist who had become Prime Minister of the newly proclaimed "Bavarian Free State" only a few months earlier. The assassination led to widespread unrest in the streets of Munich. Workers' councils—formed earlier as waves of strikes spread throughout the industrial center—decided to take control. The Bavarian Republic of Councils was proclaimed on April 7, 1919.

Factories came under the control of those who worked them and the surplus luxury homes of the rich were turned over to the homeless.

A militia was created to defend the new Republic of

19

Councils. Thousands of unemployed workers volunteered for duty, and its ranks soon swelled to 20,000. But it's existence wasn't enough to defend the fledgling revolution.

On May 3, 1919, a force of close to 40,000, made up of paramilitaries and remnants of the German army, attacked the Bavarian Republic of Councils. The bitter battle ended with the victory of the counterrevolutionaries. As the New York Times reported, the "Republic in Munich was overthrown ... by force of arms."[4] More than 1,000 supporters of the Republic of Councils were killed in the fighting and another 700 men and women were imprisoned, only to be later executed.

USSR

Probably the most well known workers' revolution of all time took place in 1917 in what was then the Russian Empire.

After the Tsar was forced to abdicate by the February Revolution, a provisional government lead by bourgeois socialists took over. At the same time, workers' councils began to spring up, with the most important council arising in Petrograd (today St. Petersburg).

The refusal of the bourgeois socialists in the provisional government to withdraw from the bloody fighting of World War I, combined with mass unemployment, a steep drop in wages, a sharp increase in the cost of living and a myriad of other factors lead the workers to revolt. In a period of two months, more than a million workers spread out across various industries went out on strike.

The provisional government's problems were compounded by thousands of peasant rebellions in the countryside. Soon, worn out soldiers and sailors began to refuse orders from those higher up the chain of command. The revolution was developing.

Numerous demonstrations of workers and soldiers soon

broke out demanding that power be taken away from the provisional government and transferred to the workers' councils.

As the provisional government weakened it resorted to increasingly harsh measures to maintain its grip on power, but even they were not enough to preserve its faltering rule. General Lavr Kornilov began moving troops towards Petrograd with the goal of taking power and preventing a workers' revolution. The Bolshevik Russian Social Democratic Labor Party (later to become the Communist Party) successfully appealed to the workers, soldiers and sailors to meet, and defeat, the coup attempt. Kornilov's scheme was rendered impossible as "The railway operators stopped his trains, the telegraph operators stopped his messages."[5]

Soon after, an uprising broke out in Tallinn, Estonia. Two days later, the Red Guards--or workplace militias--of Petrograd, acting with the mandate of well over a hundred workers' councils throughout the former Russian Empire, took over the major government buildings, culminating with the seizure of the Winter Palace. A Congress of Councils of Workers' and Soldiers' Deputies was held in order to officially transfer control to the workers' councils. The working class had taken power into its own hands.

Things quickly began to change. Control of the factories was transferred to the workers' councils, wages were raised, the working day was shortened to eight hours, banks were nationalized, church property was seized, and the new government publicly refused to make payment on foreign debts accumulated by the previous regimes.

But the workers' hold on power was tenuous to say the least. Almost immediately, counterrevolutionary forces, backed by the capitalist Allies, began to congeal. Open military attacks were to follow.

To defend itself against the counterrevolutionary White

21

Army, and subsequent invasions by fourteen foreign armies, the infant "Socialist Republic" sought to increase its military capabilities. Under the argument that a purely working class militia of the type long advocated by workers' socialism[6] would not be sufficient, the Red Guards were reorganized into a Workers' and Peasant's Red Army in a process headed by Leon Trotsky, a Bolshevik leader who had been named the People's Commissar of War.

Besides the peasants who were brought into the Red Army, a large number of military officers from the old Tsarist army were also incorporated into the newly created force as "specialists." By the end of the civil war that broke out almost immediately following the revolution, former Tsarist officers made up more than 70 percent of the command and administrative staff of the Red Army.[7] Of course, in fitting with their class position, these officers were granted special privileges.[8]

By coming under the domination and control of members of the petty-bourgeoisie, the working class Red Guard militias were transformed into an administratively controlled standing army. Thus, by the end of 1920, as the civil war had been for the most part won, the armed forces of the state had definitively fallen out of the hands of the working class.

At the same time, the workers were losing their grip elsewhere.

From 1918 onward, factory committees which had risen prior to and during the revolution were rendered ineffectual or eliminated all together, while bodies of petty-bourgeois "experts" and administrators became increasingly dominant.

Along with this came the exclusion of opposing (i.e. working class) viewpoints from official newspapers.

The workers' councils too were losing their power. Though they wouldn't be completely transformed into ceremonial bodies until 1931, and then officially discarded in

22

1936, the workers' councils had been rendered completely ineffective as organs of workers' rule by the end of 1920.

At the Ninth Congress of the Russian Communist Party, held in the Spring of 1920, Leon Trotsky argued for the militarization of labor, stating that the "The working class ... must be thrown here and there, appointed, commanded, just like soldiers."[9] Thrown, appointed and commanded by whom? By those accustomed to carrying out such tasks: the administrators!

This call for the working class to be commanded and thrown around was perfectly in line with the bureaucracy's generally paternalistic approach toward the toiling masses, which went as far as scolding workers for using "bad language" that was "stupid and ugly."[10]

Several voices were raised in the Ninth Congress and elsewhere against what was to come, but having lost control of the armed bodies of the state, not to mention many of its most dedicated and advanced individual members in the long and brutal civil war, the working class had no real means of resisting the ongoing degeneration.

The Ninth Congress passed a resolution that would lead to the replacement of direct worker control over production with individual management. By the end of the year, most vital enterprises had come under the command of petty-bourgeois administrators. Workers had become "subjected again to managerial authority, labor discipline, wage incentives, scientific management...".[11] The character of the newly congealed regime had revealed itself. "It was a dictatorship run by full-time 'cadres' or bosses...".[12]

The workers had definitively lost all control. This was perfectly illustrated in the following months as two desperate last attempts by the working class to assert itself were thwarted by the new ruling elite.

The first was the rise of the Workers' Group, led by metal worker Gavril Myasnikov. In its manifesto, this group

23

called for direct worker control of production through workers' councils and press freedom for all working people. But it was completely marginalized from the very beginning. More attention was given to the Workers' Opposition, which called for trade union control over the economy.

As Alexandra Kollontai, a proponent of the Workers' Opposition in the party pointed out: "Only the peasants gained directly by the revolution. As far as the middle classes are concerned, they very cleverly adapted themselves to the new conditions, together with the representatives of the rich bourgeoisie(!) who had occupied all the responsible and directing positions in the Soviet institutions (particularly in the sphere of directing State economy, in the industry organizations and the re-establishment of commercial relations with foreign nations). Only the basic class of the Soviet Republic, which bore all the burdens of the dictatorship as a mass, ekes out a shamefully pitiful existence."[13]

After the Tenth Congress in 1921, Myasnikov was expelled from the Russian Communist Party. In the years following he was hounded, exiled, arrested and finally executed. Many of the leading members of the Workers' Opposition abandoned their political positions and reintegrated themselves into the party.

The final major attempt by the working class to regain power and set things right came in the form of the Kronstadt Rebellion, a desperate last gasp in a powerful flood of bureaucratization.

Responding to a number of strikes occurring in Petrograd, the sailors of Kronstadt—who were widely considered heroes among the working class for their past revolutionary activities—revolted in March, 1921, demanding free speech rights for workers and peasants, the release of all workers and peasants held in prison, the equalization of rations for all, the formation of genuine workers' councils, and more. In short, they were fighting for a return to the road of the

24

proletarian revolution the best way they knew how.

Workers in several parts of Petrograd either struck or made plans to strike in support of the sailors, but organization was difficult after martial law was proclaimed by the state bureaucrats.

The Red Army was brought out to crush the Kronstadt rebellion, and after a brief but bitter fight, it finally succeeded— on the day following the fiftieth anniversary of the Paris Commune.

With the last attempts of the working class thwarted, there was no longer any question of which class ruled. The administrative class was now firmly in power in the Soviet Federated Socialist Republics, paying lip service to the proletarian revolution while simultaneously riding on the backs of the workers themselves.

* * *

When and how did this transformation happen? There's no need to seek out any premeditated plots or conspiracies. The seed of what was to grow was there all along. The petty-bourgeoisie was already accustomed to holding the reigns as Taylorism, or "scientific management," in which the administrative petty-bourgeoisie formally took over the day-to-day economic and political tasks from the capitalist owners, had become the gold standard for capitalism the world over.

And let us not forget that petty-bourgeois socialism itself existed side by side with workers' socialism since the revolutionary struggle against capitalism first began.

There's no doubt that what originally occurred in the Russian Empire in 1917 was a genuine workers' revolution. But while this revolution successfully overthrew the capitalists, and capitalism, it was isolated and unable to fully complete its tasks

25

(i.e. to integrate all sectors of society into the working class, thus eliminating classes altogether). Consequently, in the vacuum that existed in the months following the initial tumult, many of the same bureaucrats that filled the managerial and administrative positions under the Tsar again found their way into those familiar positions of leadership.

With the capitalists destroyed as a class and the means of production brought under state ownership, the administrators were no longer managing the economy for a higher capitalist ruling class. If scientific management had put the means of production under the practical control of petty-bourgeoisie administrators, it had also proved the possibility of excluding the capitalists from the equation completely. The petty-bourgeois were now able to organize production in their own interests. This economic control gave the administrators a base from which to seize political power. By 1921, they had accomplished that task.

In the years that followed, the administrators perfected their rule. The Soviet Federated Socialist Republics were officially brought together under centralized leadership as the Union of Soviet Socialist Republics (USSR). With Joseph Stalin at the helm, the petty-bourgeoisie cemented its hold on power through a series of factional struggles, changes in the economic and political structures, purges, arrests and executions. Through this process, voices sympathetic to the interests of the working class were eliminated from public life once and for all.

Instead of acting in their own interests, the workers were expected to fall in line behind the "enlightened" rulers, and they were chided—or worse—when they didn't. For example, the November 15, 1938 issue of the Communist Party's newspaper *Pravda* decried the "disparaging attitudes" workers held toward the petty-bourgeois "intelligentsia," of the type "which were widespread in the pre-Revolutionary period, when the intelligentsia served the landowners and capitalists." The Party declared that this was "savage, hooliganistic, and dangerous for the Soviet state," and thus impermissible.

Society was completely reshaped in the image of the petty-bourgeoisie. Production was centralized in a state-administered "command economy." The right of recall and the long-established practice of limiting of pay for officials to the rate received by average workers was done away with. Homosexuality and prostitution, which the revolution had decriminalized under the principle of "absolute non-interference of the state and society into sexual matters, so long as nobody is injured and no one's interests are encroached upon"[14] were again outlawed.

In what were some of the most monumental reversals, immense gains made by women through the revolution were rolled back and eliminated. Abortion, which was made legal and freely available on demand for the first time anywhere in the world three years after the revolution, was outrageously outlawed under the auspices of "the continual improvement of the material well-being of the toilers."[15] The goal of the workers' revolution, to socialize domestic chores like child care and cooking by establishing things like cafeterias and nurseries, so that women would be free to participate fully in public life, fell by the wayside. Despite their greatly improved level of education and entry *en masse* into the workforce, women workers and peasants were once again treated as domestic servants and baby-making machines. Praised for "the great and responsible duty of giving birth to and bringing up citizens," women were awarded official maternity metals for bearing large numbers of children.

"All the old crap" began to reappear throughout society. The story was no different in education, where "school uniforms reappeared, making boys and girls in Soviet high schools look very like their predecessors in Tsarist gymnasia. The reorganization of higher education was also in many respects a return to traditional, prerevolutionary norms. The old professors recovered their authority; entrance requirements

27

were once again based on academic rather than social and political criteria; and examinations, degrees and academic titles were reinstated."[16]

The international perspective of the working class, which spans the globe and has a shared interest that permeates all borders, was replaced with the narrow nationalist slogan of "socialism in one country." Rather than fight for international revolution, in order to do away with capitalism on a world scale, the petty-bourgeois rulers of the USSR sought a place for themselves in the global order by pursuing the policy of "peaceful coexistence." Patriotism and national chauvinism also reemerged as "The term *rodina* (motherland), despised by the Old Bolshevik internationalists, came back into common use."[17]

Petty-bourgeois socialism was in full effect for the first time in world history. But it couldn't last forever.

Although it may superficially utilize a few of the same forms as workers' socialism, petty-bourgeois socialism lacks its transitional character toward a higher, classless form of society. The rule of the petty-bourgeoisie is a historical dead end, and the inner economic workings of its bureaucratic form of socialism reflect that.

By the late-1980's, a period of unshakable stagnation set in throughout the USSR. The contradictions of administrative socialism had reached an apex.

Economic instability begot political inability. The system began to crumble. A section of the bureaucracy attempted in vain to keep the whole thing together, while another saw the inevitability of the system's collapse and sought out positions in the new order to come. In 1991, the Union of Soviet Socialist Republics imploded, paving the way for the reemergence of capitalism throughout its vast expanses.

Petty-bourgeois revolutions

Hungary 1919

After being soundly defeated in World War I, the Austro-Hungarian Empire collapsed. In 1918, Count Mihály Károlyi took power, but was unable to hold onto it. Károlyi's new government, representing a weak and damaged capitalist class, was completely impotent. As discontentment grew among the workers, strikes broke out, soldiers formed councils and the newly formed Communist Party grew enormously.

The reigns of power were transferred to the bourgeois socialist Social Democrats as a last ditch effort to save the capitalist system; but the they too were far too weak to rule. The Social Democrats sought out the support of the Communist Party, the only political force that was really organized and united. When the Communists, whose leaders they had imprisoned, refused to offer any outside support, the discredited Social Democrats were forced to seek out a merger between the two parties. Thus the advocates of gradual "evolutionary" reforms to bring about a socialist transformation (which in reality meant preserving capitalism indefinitely) were now prepared to join the Communists and proclaim a socialist government.

But what kind of socialist government could this be?

As one modern petty-bourgeois socialist outfit in the United Kingdom put it:

"Without a single shot being fired, with no fighting, not even a street demonstration ... The populace of Budapest woke on the morning of 22 March 1919 to find the Red Flag flying from the Parliament Building and the bourgeois democratic revolution transformed into a proletarian revolution!"[18]

30

Unless we are to believe that the working class can take power while it is--literally!--asleep, we must acknowledge that this socialist republic was not created by the workers themselves.

No, this was an example of the petty-bourgeoisie— having been inspired and instructed by the unfolding events in the Soviet Federated Socialist Republics—taking power.

Much of the popular support the new rulers were able to muster was based not on workers striving for their emancipation from capitalism but rather nationalist sentiment.

"Communist leader Bella Kun ... [was] pursuing an illusion. The support for his regime emanated not from anti-capitalist sentiments but from nationalism. By the summer ... it was clear that he was no more able to prevent the shrinkage of Hungary's borders than his predecessors has been."[19]

For this and other reasons, the Hungarian petty-bourgeois socialists did not fare nearly as well as their Russian counterparts.

Almost immediately, Hungary faced invasion from Romanian and Czechoslovakian forces. On June 16, the Hungarian Red Guards invaded Upper Hungary and proclaimed a Slovak socialist republic, but this advance was soon reversed. Romania eventually succeeded in its invasion. On August 6, the short-lived existence of the Hungarian Soviet Republic was brought to an end.

In the years following the fall of the Hungarian Soviet Republic, its leader, Bela Kun, became a prominent leader of the Communist International and an advocate of the "Theory of the Offensive," which called for an immediate all out attack on capitalist rule. Kun's advocacy of this theory, as well as his

31

previous activities in Slovakia, along with Soviet general Tukhachevsky's advocacy of "revolution from without," foreshadowed the USSR regime's future expansion-by-force of petty-bourgeois socialism into Eastern Europe following World War II.

Hungary 1944

In the build up to World War II, the Nazi Regime received a large amount of outside support from a number of the world's leading capitalists and their representatives. Seeing in Nazi Germany a battering ram with which to destroy the newly solidified regime in the USSR and pave the way for the reopening of markets throughout the wide swaths of the former Tsarist empire, many of the most powerful capitalist countries greatly assisted Hitler and his henchmen (until later, when the countries in Western Europe themselves became a target of German expansionism).

The Nazi war machine dealt extensive damage to the USSR. Indeed, no country suffered more human and material loss. But eventually, after much intense fighting, the tide was turned and the Soviet army rode into Nazi-occupied areas of Eastern Europe victoriously. The building blocks for the Eastern Bloc were laid.

* * *

The Soviet Army occupied Hungary in 1944. The means of production were subsequently nationalized and the USSR set about consolidating petty-bourgeois rule with phony elections, political maneuvering, expulsions and arrests. In 1949, the People's Republic of Hungary was established under the rule of "wise teacher" Mátyás Rákosi, a former leader of the Hungarian Soviet Republic and the Communist International.

32

The petty-bourgeois socialists perfected their rule in Hungary as they did in the USSR: with a series of show trials, purges, arrests and executions.

In 1956, the working class of Hungary revolted, setting up workers' councils and fighting for direct economic and political control. Military forces from the USSR, joined by local armed bodies, crushed the uprising. The use of the armed apparatuses *against* the workers clearly illustrated the class character of the states in Hungary and the USSR, dispelling any illusions that what existed in those countries had anything to do with working class rule.

The rule of the administrative class continued on in Hungary until the October 1989 Party Congress, when the capitalist class seized political power in the powerful wave then sweeping the Eastern Bloc.

East Germany

The Soviet Army took Berlin, the capital of Germany, in mid-1945.

As per an earlier agreement reached by the Allies, the Soviet army occupied the portion of Germany that would later be colloquially known as East Germany.

In 1949, the formation of the German Democratic Republic in East Germany was announced as the seizure of power by the petty-bourgeoisie was finalized.

Despite the existence of a more advanced economic base than what existed when the petty-bourgeoisie took took power in the Soviet Union, bureaucratic "socialism in half a country" was ultimately no more sustainable than the bureaucratic "socialism in one country" it was modeled after.

In 1953, strikes broke out across East Germany in response to increasing demands on working people. Strike committees were formed spontaneously and organized actions were carried out by workers against the newly formed petty-bourgeois socialist state. It took the force of 25,000 soldiers from the Soviet Army to crush the uprising.

Afterward, the bureaucratic rulers increased the power and reach of their state apparatus to prevent "another 1953." In the end, even this desperate attempt to stay in power proved futile.

Structural and economic problems began to emerge in East German in the 1970's. By the 1980's things broke into the open as they had elsewhere in the region.

More protests occurred in 1989. By the end of the year, petty-bourgeois rule was brought to an end. East Germany was integrated into the capitalist Federal Republic of Germany in 1990.

Bulgaria

In 1944, the Prime Minister of Bulgaria, a Nazi-puppet named Dobri Bozhilov, was overthrown in a coup backed by the USSR. Afterward, the petty-bourgeoisie immediately began to cement its grip on power.

In 1946, Bulgaria became the People's Republic of Bulgaria, with Joseph Stalin's personal friend and Communist International leader Georgi Dimitrov as its premier.

The reign of the petty-bourgeoisie in Bulgaria went on relatively unimpeded until the the late 1980's, when the internal contradictions of the system became intolerable.

Petty-bourgeois socialism was overturned in Bulgaria in 1989.

Poland

Poland was first occupied by the Soviet Army in 1944,

34

when they beat back the Nazi military forces stationed there.

The petty-bourgeoisie came to power with the helping hand of the USSR as the means of the production were brought under national ownership

As occurred elsewhere, petty-bourgeois rule was secured by means of political maneuvering, arrests and executions.

Poland officially became the People's Republic of Poland in 1952.

The working class periodically fought open battles against the bureaucratic regime.

In 1956, 1970 and 1976 as the contradictions of petty-bourgeois socialism began to be felt most sharply in Poland, workers struck in protest of poor living conditions and price rises, forcing some reforms. As the workers began to coordinate their strikes, the beginnings of a working class movement started to take shape. Here and there, struggles rose and fell. More than once, the seeds of something more were sewn, only to later rot in the soil.

In the following years, some of the remnants of the movement were organized underground, though with a different composition and mission. The prestige created in genuine working class struggles was to be hijacked by capitalist forces backed by the Western imperialist bloc and the disenfranchised hierarchy of the Catholic Church.

The final push toward change began "on July 1, 1980 when the Polish government announced massive food-price increases... The pent-up resentments among Polish workers triggered strikes throughout the country, the most important of which took place at the Lenin Shipyards in the Baltic seaport of Gdansk. There the workers closed down the yards and virtually defied the government to do anything about it. After initial vacillations, the Gdansk strikes chose fellow worker Lech Walesa as their leader and began to issue political demands as well as economic ones."[20]

35

Time and circumstances saw the Strike Committee born out of the struggle transformed into an official organization with state recognition. Capitalism found a wiling stooge in the aspirant Walesa, who secured the leading position in the new Catholic Church-backed "independent union" the Strike Committee had become.

Soon after, Solidarity--the Walesa-led union U.S. President Ronald Reagan praised while he was simultaneously smashing the air traffic controller union back in the states-- emerged as the primary force fighting for the reestablishment of capitalism in Poland.

At the end of 1989, as the transformative tide swept across Eastern Europe, petty-bourgeois socialism was overthrown in Poland and a new capitalist state was created. In 1990, Solidarity leader Lech Walesa became the first president of the new Poland.

Romania

The Soviet Army occupied Romania in 1944, after driving the Nazis from the country's borders.

Petty-bourgeois rule was consolidated in Romania in the typical fashion, although the final results were a bit different in form.

In 1947, Romania officially became a "People's Republic."

When Romanian leader Gheorghe Gheorghiu-Dej died in 1965, party bureaucrat Nicolae Ceauşescu became first secretary of the Romanian Workers Party. Fresh in office, Ceauşescu changed the name of the organization to the Romanian Communist Party and proclaimed the country a "Socialist Republic." The next twenty-four years were marked by the peculiarities of his unique brand of top-down leadership.

Ceauşescu's openness to foreign relations with the

36

capitalist powers and partial political independence from Moscow was overshadowed by his autocratic regime's methods and the cult of personality he fostered at home. Ceauşescu's Romania was as rigid as the strongmen he looked up to.

In 1989, the contradictions of petty-bourgeois socialism throughout Eastern Europe and the pressures of paying back loans taken out from the capitalist bankers of the International Monetary Fund led to rationing and shortages of food and other necessities. Things soon reached the breaking point. A revolt broke out in December that would culminate in the overthrow of petty-bourgeois rule in Romania, and the public execution of General Secretary Nicolae Ceauşescu and his wife.

Czechoslovakia

Although Czechoslovakia had one of the largest and most popular communist parties in the world before World War II, capitalist rule was replaced with the rule of the petty-bourgeoisie there in much the same way that it had been in the rest of the countries ripped from the hands of the Nazis by the Soviet Army.

In 1948, Czechoslovakia officially became the People's Republic of Czechoslovakia.

Czechoslovakia took the same path followed by the rest of the Eastern Bloc, with nationalizations and centralized control by state bureaucrats. And just as they had in the rest of the Eastern Bloc, the contradictions of petty-bourgeois rule led to political instability in Czechoslovakia.

Economic decline in the 1960's resulted in the rise of an influential faction in the bureaucracy that sought a way out of the stagnation. After Alexander Dubček became First Secretary of the Communist Party of Czechoslovakia in 1968, his regime enacted a series of liberalizing reforms during a period that became known as the Prague Spring. After the leadership of the Soviet Union proved unable to turn back the sweeping changes through diplomatic means, soldiers from the USSR, Bulgaria, Poland and Hungary invaded Czechoslovakia and removed the reformists from their positions in the state. The dominance of the petty-bourgeois socialists was firmly reestablished.

Before long, unrest once again began to occur throughout the country. The inability of the bureaucratic socialist system to meet the basic needs of the population worsened. State repression was unable to stop either the external pressures of the capitalist world or domestic discontent.

As 1989 drew to a close so did administrative rule in Czechoslovakia. Alexander Dubček found a comfortable position for himself as a leading politician in the new government formed after the restoration of capitalism. The country itself was split in two in 1993, resulting in the creation of the Czech Republic and Slovakia.

Yugoslavia

The petty-bourgeoisie seized power in Yugoslavia in the midst of World War II.

Partisan fighters, lead by administrative socialist Josip Broz Tito, battled the German and Italian occupation forces throughout the duration of the war. In 1944, the partisans took the capital with the assistance of the Soviet Army. By the end of 1945, the occupiers had been driven from the borders of Yugoslavia.

Josip Broz's "People's Front" formed a government and the Federal People's Republic of Yugoslavia was created.

The origins of the new republic differed from those of the People's Democracies, but the results were the same.

Despite refusing to the follow the lead of the USSR's rulers, due more to narrow nationalist concerns on the part of both parties than any real ideological quibbles, petty-bourgeois socialism in Yugoslavia strongly resembled the original Soviet

38

model at its base.

Schemes like "workers' self-management" emerged in Yugoslavia in subsequent years, but they were no more effective than other models utilized across the Eastern Bloc in propping up bureaucratic socialism.

Economic problems begin to emerge in the 1980's. Contradictions built until the end of 1989, when petty-bourgeois rule finally gave way.

Mongolia

In 1921, the Mongolian People's Party—a petty-bourgeois socialist outfit founded as the petty-bourgeoisie finalized its seizure of power in the Russian Empire—took Mongolia with the aid of the Red Army.

The petty-bourgeoisie immediately set about establishing its rule.

In 1924, the formation of the Mongolian People's Republic was announced.

The bureaucrats ruled Mongolia until 1990. As the associated Eastern Bloc crumbled in Europe in 1989, mass demonstrations broke out in the capital city of Ulaanbaator. By the middle of the following year, petty-bourgeois socialism had fallen and many individual administrators had found comfortable places for themselves in the new capitalist system.

China

In 1949, the Communist Party of China took power after years of battling Japanese occupation forces and the nationalist Kuomintang organization. The victory of the "Communists" and founding of the People's Republic of China marked the seizure of power by the petty-bourgeoisie in China.

As the national capitalist class had proven too weak to create a modern Chinese republic, the petty-bourgeoisie stepped forward and asserted themselves. After gaining the upper hand in a long civil war, the People's Liberation Army was able to take Beijing without even fighting a battle.

The establishment of workers' socialism requires the working class to take control of the means of production and establish its own forms of rule. This never occurred in China. In fact, there wasn't much in the way of working class participation in the Chinese Revolution at all.

Instead, the Chinese petty-bourgeois socialists came to power on the backs of the restless peasant masses.

This was no aberration. The working class made up only about one percent of the total population of China in 1949. At the time of the revolution, "China's basic social conflict was rural. The two opposing sides were the peasant masses and the landed upper class. Alongside the dire poverty and exploitation suffered by immense numbers of peasants, all other problems seemed minor."[21]

Subsequently, "the proletariat played a negligible role in the last and decisive phase of the revolution. Neither major strikes nor urban uprisings paved the way for the Red Army ... There were very few workers in the triumphant Red Army; it was composed essentially of peasants and officered by other peasants and [petty-bourgeois] intellectuals."[22]

But even though the petty-bourgeois socialists came to power by harnessing a largely peasant struggle, they still had to reorganize the economy in their own interests. Thus, once the revolution was consolidated, a campaign was waged to industrialize the country and bring agriculture under state control. The collectivization of farm lands was the hallmark of socialization in China.

Existing industry was also brought in line with the new system. So, "most companies making heavy industrial goods were nationalized, too, although their owners were often kept on as managers."[23]

In their attempt to transform agrarian China into a modern country and perfect their variety of petty-bourgeois socialism by fiat, the administrators launched one blundering campaign after another—from the misnamed "Great Leap Forward," in which the greatest mobilization of human beings the world had ever known was carried out in a failed attempt to rapidly advance the national economy, to the even less aptly titled "Great Proletarian Cultural Revolution," which was in reality nothing more than a particularly brutal factional struggle waged at the expense of the general population.

Despite all of the mismanagement, the fact that real, world-historic advances were made in areas like life expectancy and literacy cannot be denied. Still, it was not enough.

Eventually, bureaucratic socialism in China began to run out of steam. As had occurred elsewhere, the internal contradictions of the system itself led to its disintegration.

After years of crisis, things really began to give way in the late 1970's. This phenomenon increased in the years that followed. Sensing what was to come, and wanting to avoid the fate of the petty-bourgeois rulers who were unceremoniously forced from power elsewhere, many of the ruling bureaucrats in China sought a way out for themselves through the introduction of a capitalist economy which they could administer. A storm began to brew within the ruling bureaucracy, between those who wanted an escape and those who refused to abandon petty-bourgeois rule. Before long, it would break out into the open.

The Tianamen Square Massacre of 1989, which was followed by a series of arrests, executions and purges, definitively marked the overturn of petty-bourgeois socialism and the coming to power of the capitalist class in China. To prevent outright disintegration like that seen in the Eastern Bloc, key state-owned industries and positions in the

41

bureaucracy were preserved for elements of the petty-bourgeoisie.

Albania

In Albania, the petty-bourgeoisie seized power in the aftermath of World War II. Partisans, led by Enver Hoxha, defeated the fascist occupation without the direct assistance of the Soviet army, leading to the formation of the Socialist People's Republic of Albania in 1946.

For the next several decades, Albania was lead by the Party of Labor of Albania (PLA), which was founded in 1941 as the Communist Party of Albania with "about 200 members, mostly students and young intellectuals."[24]

The class relations in Albania, which was among the most economically backward countries in Europe, meant that petty-bourgeois rule took on a particularly incestuous form. Thirteen years after the foundation of the Party, "more than half of the 53 members of the Central Committee of the PLA were related."[25]

With the petty-bourgeoisie firmly in power, society was reorganized from above on terms best suited to the new ruling class. In 1955, individual private farms produced the vast majority of the country's agricultural output. Within five years, the majority of the largely rural country's agricultural output came from cooperative and state-owned farms directly controlled by the petty-bourgeois administrators.

Several plans were also launched in an attempt to industrialize the country, but their success was greatly limited by the economic condition of the country and the isolation imposed upon it after the ruling bureaucracy broke with the rest of Socialist Bloc over issues of national interest (which were of course couched in ideological terms, with all the usual books and speeches).

42

Petty-bourgeois socialism in Albania was modeled on the original "war-footed" Stalinist regime in the Soviet Union. This extensive emulation manifested itself widely: from the holding of show trials to the creation of an extensive cult of personality around "Supreme Comrade" Enver Hoxha. And even though women made great strides in areas like employment and education in what was previously one of the most patriarchal societies in the world, "In practice it was in their traditional role as mothers that women were most prized under the Hoxha regime, just as they had been in prewar days. For producing 6 children a Mother's Medal was awarded; for nine, the Glory Medal and for 12, the Heroine Mother's Medal."[26]

Petty-bourgeois rule came to an end in Albania in 1991. With their brand of socialism collapsing all around them, many of the Albanian bureaucrats sought out a deal with capitalist forces to maintain their positions of privilege in the new order.

North Korea

Korea was annexed by imperialist Japan in 1910. Until its defeat in the closing battles of World War II, Japan continued to control Korea by way of an incredibly brutal occupation.

After Japan's defeat, the U.S. and the USSR reached an agreement that each country would occupy one-half of the Korean Peninsula while preparations for the formation of a new national government were made. The interests of each power were in play all along.

Koreans quickly established a provisional government on their own, but the U.S. refused to recognize it, fearing "Communist influence."

Instead, a section of the U.S. military governed the southern half of Korea, with the assistance of the same Koreans collaborators who helped administer the country under the Japanese occupation. Japanese officials themselves remained in the southern half of Korea under the watchful eye of the U.S. military rulers until 1946.

A new government was eventually established via a sham election in 1948 which was boycotted by popular opposition parties and held only in the U.S.-occupied part of Korea. Syngman Rhee, a virulent proponent of capitalism who had recently returned from the U.S., emerged as the president of South Korea.

Propped-up by the U.S. military forces in the region, Rhee's government carried out a bloody campaign of terror against workers and farmers under the banner of "eliminating communism." Some 100,000 Korean men, women and children lost their lives while countless others were brutally tortured.

Meanwhile, in the northern part of the Korean peninsula, a temporary "Civil Authority" under the Soviet Army was set up in 1945, while "provisional committees" were established across the region. Property owned by Japanese capitalists and their collaborators, along with all key industries, were nationalized. Capitalism was overturned as the petty-bourgeois bureaucrats took power.

In 1946, the creation of a Provisional People's Committee was proclaimed, with petty-bourgeois socialist Kim Il-Sung – a leader of the guerrilla war against the Japanese occupation – at its head. Two years later, the Soviet army withdrew from Korea.

Several days after Syngman Rhee unilaterally proclaimed the Republic of Korea (ROK) in the south on August 15, 1948, Kim Il-Sung proclaimed the Democratic People's Republic of Korea (DPRK) in the north. The petty-bourgeoisie has remained in power in North Korea since— withstanding devastating war between the Koreas, natural disaster and isolation—though their future becomes increasingly bleaker by the day.

The DPRK was hit especially hard by the collapse of the

Eastern Bloc. Having already fallen drastically since the late-1970's, when the South began to surpass it economically, the loss of its key trade partners caused North Korea to stumble even further. The chain of events put the whole system of petty-bourgeois rule in peril. Things have only continued to worsen since.

The ruling bureaucracy realizes this, of course, and has begun to search for an escape. References to "Marxism-Leninism," the official dogma of the old Socialist Bloc, have been abandoned in favor of *Juche*, a nationalist doctrine concocted by Kim Il-Sung and further developed by his son and current head-of-state Kim Jong-Il. The latter's *Songun*, or "military first" policy, which first emerged in the 1990's, has replaced all pretenses of working class rule with direct references to the "leading role" of the armed forces. Today, all mentions of communism have been removed from the constitution and the official website of the DPRK promotes investment by promising "highly qualified, loyal and motivated personnel" at "the lowest labor cost in Asia."

"As opposed to other Asian countries," the petty-bourgeois rulers ensure capitalists looking to invest that workers in the DPRK "will not abandon their positions for higher salaries once they are trained." Furthermore, they promise that the country "will become in the next years the most important hub for trading in North-East Asia."[27]

The infamously bizarre aspects of North Korean society directly correspond to the country's isolation and embattlement. Attempts by the petty-bourgeois rulers to escape these conditions have not fared well so far. There are few options left for the bureaucracy. If the international situation does not change enough to allow the DPRK to take the "Chinese road" to capitalism, the regime will eventually collapse, either under its own weight or by the bloody hands of one or another set of capitalist rulers.

45

Viet Nam

The French imperialists took control of Vietnam in a series of military invasions that began in 1859 and concluded in 1885. Despite a number of peasant uprisings, the French continued to rule Viet Nam until it was taken over by the Japanese imperialists in their expansionist drive during World War II.

The Japanese invaders were fought by partisans of the Viet Nam Doc Lap Dong Minh Hoi (Viet Minh, or League for the Independence of Vietnam). These fighters received limited support from the U.S. imperialists, who at the time were battling the Japanese for control of lands in and around the Pacific Ocean.

The defeat of the Japanese in the war created a power vacuum in Viet Nam. The Viet Minh, which was dominated by petty-bourgeois socialists led by Ho Chi Minh, found itself in control of large parts of the country. In 1945, the Democratic Republic of Viet Nam was proclaimed, thus marking the assumption of power by the petty-bourgeoisie.

After a period of regrouping following the end of World War II, the French imperialists attempted to retake Viet Nam by force with extensive assistance from the United States. When that failed, the United States attempted to turn Viet Nam back into a dependent imperialist possession directly. After a long and bitter war in which the imperialists maimed and killed millions and leveled the country with bombings and biological weapons, the U.S. forces were also driven from Viet Nam.

In 1975, the forces of the Democratic Republic of Viet Nam took Saigon, the capital of the state established in the south of Viet Nam by the imperialists and their local puppets.

After the petty-bourgeoisie cemented its hold on power on a national scale, remaining land and businesses were taken out of the hands of private owners and brought under the control of the state. The Vietnamese economy was administered in accordance with the model of bureaucratic socialism practiced in the USSR.

But the petty-bourgeois administrators proved unable to resurrect the Vietnamese economy from its shallow grave, dug by years of war, colonialism and underdevelopment. Soon after reuniting the country under their rule, these bureaucrats were forced to make changes that ultimately weakened their position.

At the Sixth Congress of the Communist Party, held in 1986, the old representatives of the petty-bourgeoisie were removed from power by "reformers" who sought to improve the condition of the economy.

An economic policy known as "doi moi" (renovation) was subsequently implemented. State control of the economy was loosened, a stock market was created, foreign investment and the establishment of capitalist enterprises was encouraged, and state-owned enterprises and banks were sold off to the highest bidder.

Petty-bourgeois socialism was falling apart internationally and had proven unworkable locally. A number of bureaucrats began to maneuver and seek places for themselves in a new, capitalist Viet Nam.

In 1991, at the Seventh Congress of the Communist Party, a huge number of the members of the party's ruling Central Committee and Politburo were replaced. Do Muoi, a strong advocate of the new capitalist market economy, was named Secretary-General.

What was then called the biggest leadership shake up in modern times marked the replacement of old petty-bourgeois bureaucrats with pro-capitalist forces that aimed to reconstruct the state to reflect the new predominant property relations.

Laos

In the years between 1893 and 1904, the French

47

imperialists took control of the fractured remains of the Lao kingdom of Lan Xang out of the hands of the Kingdom of Siam (now Thailand).

The largely peasant population of Laos periodically rebelled against the French as it had previously done against the Siamese, but always to no avail.

The Japanese occupied Laos, along with the rest of Indochina, during World War II. After the Japanese were defeated and driven from the area in 1945, the local rulers declared Laos an independent state.

But a year later, the French imperialists reoccupied Laos. Their renewed rule continued until their subsequent defeat in Indochina in 1954.

The petty-bourgeois socialist movements of Laos and Viet Nam cooperated closely. Vietnamese supply lines, including the famous "Ho Chi Minh Trail," ran through Laos. During the Vietnamese war against the U.S. invaders and their allies, the U.S. dropped more bombs on Laos than had been dropped on any other country in the history of warfare. The small impoverished country was completely devastated.

In 1975, after years of bombing and civil war, the petty-bourgeois socialist Lao People's Revolutionary Party defeated the government forces, overthrew King Savang Vatthana and took power. Thus, the Lao People's Democratic Republic was founded, with Prince Souphanouvong, son of the last vice-king of the Lao city of Luang Prabang, acting as its ceremonial leader.

Laos had no real working class to speak of. Some 90 percent of the people within its borders were subsidence farmers. Laotian socialism reflected this reality. The socialization of Laos primarily meant the taking of agricultural land into state ownership.

The establishment of petty-bourgeois socialism in Laos did not translate to economic recovery or growth. To be sure, advances were made in healthcare and education, but there was little overall progress to speak of.

As in neighboring China, petty-bourgeois socialism began to fall apart in Laos in the late-1970's. Facing multiple insurgencies and a crumbling economy, the bureaucratic rulers loosened their control of the economy and introduced rudimentary elements of the market.

In 1986, things degraded further when the government enacted the "New Economic Mechanism," introducing market reforms, lifting economic restrictions, and encouraging the creation of capitalist enterprises. The planned economy was being transformed into a capitalist market economy.

In 1991, the capitalist class took power and reorganized the state to reflect its mode of production. The "old guards" of petty-bourgeois socialism were replaced and a new constitution was drafted in which Laos was transformed into a presidential republic and the new, capitalist economy was enshrined in law.

Cambodia

The attempt at instituting petty-bourgeois socialism in Kampuchea resulted in nothing short of an absolute human catastrophe.

As was the case with Laos, the war in neighboring Viet Nam significantly overlapped into Kampuchea.

After several years of civil war, the bureaucratic Communist Party of Kampuchea (commonly known as the Khmer Rouge) took control of the capital city of Phnom Penh in 1975, marking its ascendancy to power.

The leading body of the Communist Party was made up almost entirely of French-educated petty-bourgeois students. The top-down, administrative nature of their organization was clearly illustrated by the fact that *they did even officially announce the existence of the Communist Party until two years*

49

after they had taken power!

Rejecting the role of the working class, which only made up a small portion of the population of Cambodia at the time, the Party leadership instead insisted that it was the peasantry which was the truly revolutionary force.

The policies of the new regime reflected the rural, agricultural society it grew out of as much as its idealization of peasant life. As Pol Pot, the notorious leader of the Khmer Rouge, put it, "...the peasants were the overwhelming majority of the population. They were exploited by all classes... Among all the contradictions within Kampuchean society, the contradictions which played the dominant role was that between the peasants and the landlords, because the peasantry represented the overwhelming majority, 85%, of the population. From whom did the peasants suffer exploitation? It had to be a priority to resolve this principal contradiction in order to mobilize the forces of the peasantry, who were the greatest force... That is how we defined our tasks in the democratic revolution... To liberate the peasants, who make up 85% of the population, is to liberate all the people at one blow... This was the key problem, the fundamental problem which was definitive for victory. Such was the conclusion of our analysis and such was our conviction."[28] In practice, the whole ordeal was as farcical as it was tragic.

The peasants were disdainful toward the cities for drawing the best and brightest away from the countryside. Thus, urban dwellers were put to work on rural farms. The peasantry associated the practice of modern medicine, formal education and industry with French imperialism. Subsequently, hospitals, schools and factories were closed, city dwellers lacking farming skills and individuals who were or who appeared to be educated were persecuted, and emphasis was placed upon wiping out the past, 'starting over from scratch,' and turning Kampuchea into an 'agricultural paradise.'

The awful conditions existing in Indochina at the time

also played a major role in what unfolded. Evacuating wholes cities can seem more or less rational when facing massive carpet bombing campaigns from the mightiest military in the world.

* * *

The transition to a classless society requires means capable of creating the things people need and want in abundance. Any attempts lacking this fundamentally requirement will only end up with "socialized poverty."

Though some industry developed in Cambodia in the 1950's and 60's, the Communist Party of Kampuchea took control of an extremely backward country left in a ruinous state by years upon years of colonialism and war.

The ridiculous attempt by Pol Pot and the rest of the administrative leadership of the Communist Party to not only mechanically apply aspects of revolutions that took place in countries in more advanced stages of development to Kampuchea, but also to attempt to "out do" them only aggravated things further.

The capitalist French Revolution did away with the monarchy and introduced a new calendar, declaring the start of "Year I," which was meant to represent a new beginning. Pol Pot and company emptied the cities and sent their inhabitants to the countryside, decreeing the beginning of "Year Zero," representing an attempt to roll back the clock of history.

The regimes in the USSR and China collectivized farm land and introduced mechanized implements in an attempt to modernize and improve agricultural production. The Kampuchean regime created communal rice paddies which the population was forced to work by hand.

All of this was aimed at forging something out of

nothing, immediately--typical of those accustomed to ordering from on high. With inspiration from nearby China and the kind of arrogance that is to be expected of intellectuals and national chauvinists, the Kampuchean bureaucrats proclaimed their intention to launch "The Super Great Leap Forward.... a big leap, beyond all reality."

The ruling party had a tendency to prey upon its self too. The paranoid group around Pol Pot, which had spent significant time in isolation carrying out clandestine maneuvers, was constantly seeking out challengers to its rule. When bloody purges of party members who actually conspired and even took action to overthrow the group and put an end its excesses proved insufficient, Pol Pot's Central Committee simply invented new enemies from thin air.

Throughout the period of its dominance, the Pol Pot group vehemently pushed nationalist anti-Vietnamese poison, culminating in attacks on Vietnamese residents and the eventual cross border raids into Viet Nam in late 1978 that would result in the regime's ultimate downfall.

The Vietnamese rulers—already angered by previous attacks on Vietnamese territories and citizens and the increasing number of refugees flooding across the border—responded to the 1978 invasion by storming into Kampuchea with the assistance of the "National United Front for the Salvation of Kampuchea" (FUNSK), made up largely of former members of the Communist Party who opposed the Pol Pot clique.

In a matter of days, the Vietnamese forces and FUNSK had taken the capital. The Communist Party of Kampuchea was driven from power and a new "People's Republic of Kampuchea" was established.

What remained of Pol Pot's party continued to wage war on the new regime by means of guerrilla military operations in the countryside, but it did not prevail. It later joined forces with royalist and pro-imperialist forces backed by Thailand and the

United States in a failed bid for power.

In 1989, as the market economy continued to make strong inroads in Vietnam, home of the Kampuchean regime's sponsors, a number of changes were announced for Kampuchea as well. The name of both the country and the military, the flag, national anthem, and military symbols were changed; Buddhism was declared the national religion; and capital punishment was eliminated. On top of these changes, laws were enacted encouraging individual ownership of the means of production and declaring a "free market orientation;" changes were made to the constitution defining the country as a non-aligned, neutral state; and the government announced that it would hold negotiations with the aforementioned opposition coalition.

In 1991, as the capitalists took power in Vietnam and neighboring Laos, the ruling party in Kampuchea officially rejected "Communism" and elections were scheduled to fill the seats in the newly formed government, with King Norodom Sihanouk at its head.

Somalia

Somalia, previously divided into two separate parts, officially gained independence from the United Kingdom and Italy in 1960. Somalia maintained a nominally democratic government for the next few years, though its economy and politics lagged severely.

When Abdirashid Ali Shermarke, the second President of Somalia, was assassinated in 1969, the petty-bourgeoisie lost all confidence in the fledgling rulers and decided to make a move on its own.

In the midst of the power vacuum left by the assassination, Chief of Police Jama Korshel, Major General Salaad Gabeyre Kediye and Vice Commander General Siad Barre – who openly admired the USSR after having met Soviet military officers in joint training exercises – seized power in a bloodless coup.

Barre headed the Supreme Revolutionary Council, which broke up the neocolonial state and founded a new Somali Democratic Republic under the direct rule of the local petty-bourgeoisie.

The Council legitimized its rule by claiming adherence to "scientific socialism," Siad Barre's homespun hodgepodge based on select passages lifted from socialist texts and the Qur'an. In reality, the regime differed from other bureaucratic socialist outfits only in its minutiae. The new rulers were able to gain the support of their petty-bourgeois counterparts in the USSR and the rest of the Socialist Bloc, greatly helping to prop up their new state.

The bureaucrats carried out their mission of modernization with due haste. A national language and script was adopted and a program of national education was instituted. Banks and existing industry were nationalized and new cooperative farms and factories were created under state control. Remnants of the old feudal system were uprooted and development occurred at a relatively rapid pace.

But overall, bureaucratic socialism was as limited as it was short-lived in Somalia.

The Somali military was defeated by Ethiopian forces after Barre's petty-bourgeois regime attempted to unite all Somali-inhabited parts of the Horn of Africa by force. This loss represented the beginning of the end for the ruling bureaucracy.

The USSR and the rest of the petty-bourgeois socialist countries abandoned their support of Somalia after the failed military attempt. The Somali regime subsequently looked to the United States for support and began carrying out economic and political reforms meant to meet the demands of international capitalism. It was a case of letting thieves in the back door to prevent an all out raid through the front.

Eventually, the contradictions inherent in this

relationship caught up to Barre and company. The ruler's popularity fell as misery spread throughout Somalia.

As the regime weakened, it resorted to increased bureaucratic measures and repression, as was to be expected. But as was the case elsewhere, this was not enough to prevent its downfall.

Rebellions broke out across the country. In 1991, warlord forces invaded the capital, defeated the military and overthrew the petty-bourgeois rulers.

Somalia subsequently shattered along factional lines based in the feudal past as all remaining gains of the revolution disappeared into the darkness of chaos that continues to envelope the area to this day.

Ethiopia

In Ethiopia, a committee of military officers originally assembled to respond to grievances among soldiers and investigate corruption among high ranking officials took power in 1974, imprisoning Emperor Haile Selassie and other political leaders and breaking up the old state in the process. Seizing upon the popular discontent of the downtrodden masses and the support of the radical intelligentsia, the military officers were able to carry out a revolutionary transformation of Ethiopian society.

This committee, known as the Dergue, followed the lead of the petty-bourgeois socialist states already in existence and proclaimed allegiance to "Marxism-Leninism," thus winning the political and military support of the rulers in Moscow.

Almost immediately upon coming to power, the Dergue attempted to reorganize society to the best of its abilities.

Under a program known as "land to the tiller," rural land was taken out of the hands of landlords and made national property. Industry, financial institutions, urban land holdings and rental properties were also nationalized.

In true bureaucratic faction, the Dergue ran things completely from above, either directly or via its own appointees. "The Dergue did little to improve the position of the working class; no minimum wage or social security measures were enacted. The Dergue was hostile to the labor movement's objective of organizational autonomy. In time, the Dergue imposed a leadership of its own choice over the union."[29]

Lacking a strong social base and facing growing resistance from both local and international forces, the ruling committee attempted to strengthen itself by means of dictates and increased military spending. This only led to more problems and instability.

A widespread famine that hit Ethiopia in 1984 and 85 pushed things to the breaking point. The Dergue was never able to recover.

Coming under increasing pressure and locked in battle with strengthening insurgencies, the government was reorganized in 1987. But the more things changed, the more they stayed the same. Haile Mengistu, leader of the Dergue, continued on as president even after the reorganization.

As aid from the crumbling USSR-centered Socialist Bloc petered out and the insurgencies grew, the death knell sounded for the administrative regime in Ethiopia.

In 1991, Mengistu was forced to flee the country. The government fell and the capitalist class took power. Ethiopia was reintegrated into the global economy as a dependent hub of the most powerful capitalist countries.

Cuba

In 1959, a cross-class alliance successfully overthrew the decrepit regime of Fulgencio "The Butcher" Batista, the U.S.-backed dictator of Cuba, after years of revolutionary war.

56

The alliance was indisputably led by the July 26 Movement, a broad national-front with a socialist leadership intent on breaking Cuba free from the yoke of U.S. imperialism, something the feeble national capitalists and their bureaucrat sycophants proved totally incapable of accomplishing. In Cuba, "capitalism was absentee-owned, foreign-controlled and quasi-colonial... The so-called Cuban capitalist class was dependent on American capitalism—politically, militarily, economically.... They stayed in power because they had a military regime... They were illegitimate in the eyes of virtually the entire population because they had shown their incapacity to rule effectively."[30]

As the revolution continued to advance, the leadership saw that the only way to preserve their existing accomplishments and enact the further changes they desired was to move forward, making inroads against U.S. imperialism and even those among the local capitalist class who supported the fight against the inept Batista.

As the revolution set about nationalizing the means of production--including the vast array of plantations controlled by North American capitalists--the remaining elements of the native capitalist class, the bureaucrats who served them, and much of the old petty-bourgeoisie flaked off like dead skin. They soon found an inviting home in Miami.

Along with the Batista camp and the U.S. imperialists stung by the Cuban Revolution's expropriations, many of these elements began actively plotting the overthrow of the new regime in a display of utter depravity that has yet to end.

Petty-bourgeois socialism in Cuba can be said to be unique in its specific characteristics, but it is nonetheless based on the control of nationalized means of production by the petty-bourgeoisie.

While China and Viet Nam have been accepted into the capitalist world economy, Cuba is still condemned and attacked by the major capitalist powers for refusing to abandon its form of socialism. At the same time, it has found new trading partners in capitalist regimes in South America that are currently seeking to assert some degree of independence from the U.S. and Europe in order to better their own positions.

Cuba's future then remains uncertain. But one thing is for sure. The bureaucracy in Cuba can only hold onto power for so long. The question of which class will take control in the future has yet to be decided.

National–democratic revolutions

Capitalism was ushered into existence by a series of capitalist revolutions. The first capitalist countries experienced rapid growth and expansion, which, combined with their need to search out new raw materials, labor and markets, led to their rise to positions of global dominance.

As those "old" capitalist countries grew in power, their international economic, political and military dominance combined with the nature of the global capital system itself to retard the establishment of the same kinds of capitalist economies elsewhere. Development spread at an uneven pace throughout the rest of the world. Huge cities emerged complete with modern factories only minutes away from agricultural plots farmed by individuals using ancient methods and tools from the distant past. Corporations laid claim to natural resources in far-away lands and established global supply chains, constructing roads and other infrastructure that rose alongside masses of broken-down shacks.

Even when the national capitalists were able to step forward in the underdeveloped countries (either with the support of the "old" capitalist powers or on the backs of workers, proprietors, and peasants who gave their support and sacrificed in return for promises of improvement), their attempts at moving forward fell flat.

But the existence of the USSR, a former backwater transformed into a modern power under the helmsmanship of petty-bourgeois socialists, encouraged the petty-bourgeoisie in some of the undeveloped countries to seize control with the goal of breaking their countries out of positions of subservience and backwardness and bettering their own conditions. In the view of these petty-bourgeois elements, this was immensely preferable to serving the national and international capitalists who had nothing to offer them.

In power, the petty-bourgeois bureaucrats were often able to carry out some generally progressive measures—however distorted. This served to gain them some amount of support. But as a class with no future, the petty-bourgeoisie was unable to break from the global capitalist system. Some realized this and did their best to direct capitalist development independently while others pursued "non-capitalist" or even "socialist" paths. In the end, it didn't matter. On the road to nowhere from the start, all of these regimes eventually crashed and burned.

There is perhaps no better example of this sort of disintegration than the case of Daniel Ortega. The leader of the Sandanista National Liberation Front, which lead the revolutionary war that overthrew the hated U.S.-backed Somoza dictatorship in Nicaragua in 1979, Ortega now claims to have lost Communism and found God. In Practice, he has "become a God-fearing free marketeer in cowboy trousers and white shirt with a proclivity for throwing white flowers in the air."[31] Since 2006, when he was reelected chief executive of the capitalist state, the reborn Christian Socialist has overseen a complete ban of abortion in Nicaragua. Ortega now favorably compares his "spiritual revolution" with the reactionary Islamist regime in Iran.

* * *

Karl Marx, who was the first person to really closely examine class society and the struggle for human emancipation, once wrote that "Every giant ... presupposes a dwarf, every genius a hidebound philistine.... The first are too great for this world, and so they are thrown out. But the latter strike root in it and remain.... Caesar the hero leaves behind him the play-acting Octavianus, Emperor Napoleon the bourgeois king Louis Philippe...".

61

Just as is the case when using a photo copier, the duplicate copy that follows is never as strong as the original source. This tendency could certainly be noted in the Great Revolutions of the 20th century.

What the capitalist class was no longer willing to do, the still-growing working class proved not yet able to do. The conditions for bourgeois revolution had passed and the conditions for proletarian revolution had not fully matured. The petty-bourgeoisie stepped up when the opportunity arose but ultimately, and tellingly, proved unable to administer society on its own behalf. Thus was the story of the major upheavals of the last hundred years. Elements of the petty-bourgeoisie led socialist, national-democratic and national liberation struggles which did not, and could not, result in anything that could properly be described as socialism, democracy or national liberation.

The evidence is right there, in modern Chile, Tanzania, Venezuela, Myanmar, El Salvador, etc.

Conclusion

So, *has* socialism failed? The answer depends on which of the socialisms is being referring to.

Is it the bourgeois socialism of the capitalists? This socialism has succeeded only in that it has helped the capitalist class successfully cling to power time and time again.

Or are you referring to the bureaucratic socialism of the petty-bourgeoisie? At best this form of socialism has brought significant improvements, along the lines of those brought about by the earlier capitalist revolutions, to the lives of millions of people at times and in places where the capitalist system proved impotent. At worst it ended in outright human tragedy. It allowed the petty-bourgeoisie to temporarily prevent the ruin of their class, but at the same time had the overall effect of helping to extend the existence of class society, and ultimately, capitalism as a global system.

Of course it's obvious that neither of these forms of socialism has lead to the creation of a classless society in which humanity can freely flourish; a truly human community. And since that is the point, the answer for the overwhelming majority of the world's population – those many who must toil so that the few can prosper – is that both of the aforementioned socialisms are indeed miserable failures.

But what of workers' socialism? This socialism has gone relatively untested. Where it has emerged it has succeeded only as long as it was able to survive.

This is the socialism that emerged in 1871, 1877, 1917, 1919, 1936, 1956, 1968, etc.

This is the socialism that the exploiting and oppressing classes attempt to bury underneath heaps of disparagement which is only truly deserved by the very worst of the bureaucratic and bourgeois varieties. This is the socialism that we must rediscover in practice, in order to emancipate ourselves, and in the process, liberate all of humanity.

But since the term socialism has become so indelibly identified with the rule of bureaucrats and capitalists, workers' socialism no longer need to be said to be socialism at all. Whatever its name, or whether or not it comes with any labels at all, is irrelevant.

* * *

Capitalism is an outmoded system. The means exist to provide each person on earth with the things that they need and want, from modern technology to quality housing, education and healthcare. But instead of acting in accord with the requirements of human beings, this irrational system continues its blind pursuit of profit, which is funneled into increasingly few hands.

Capitalism proves more with each passing day that it has become a fetter on human development. Unable to solve even the problems of its own creation – unemployment, war, starvation, growing inequality, the destruction of the natural environment, etc. – this system is an obstacle to the progress of our species.

Struggles break out all around on us on a near-daily basis. Revolutionary change is undoubtedly on the horizon. If it is to deliver humanity from an otherwise inevitable decent into savagery, the coming revolution will be a genuinely bottom-up revolution *against* capitalism and all forms of exploitation and oppression.

This revolution will not only move against the powerful capitalists that own the mines, oil fields, gas reserves, transportation fleets, factories, retail and wholesale chains, banks, financial monopolies media conglomerates, and other means of production and distribution. No, this revolution will go all the way in reshaping society. It will move against the landlords who exploit the human need for shelter for their own material gain and evict renters when they can no longer afford to pay; the "small business owners" who exploit basic needs by raising prices on goods people require the most; the military officers who lead workers off to die in wars that they have no vested interest in; the cops, prison guards and private security agents who beat, arrest, imprison, fine, and spy, who break strikes and hunt down those forced by their desperate conditions to take alternative "illegal" actions to survive; the managers and foremen who treat workers like robots, drag them around like a bag of bolts, and force them to sacrifice their bodies and minds to the company, all the while wielding the threat of unemployment like a stick; the union bureaucrats who act as labor-force managers and sell out the workers they supposedly represent by ditching solidarity, breaking strikes and making sweetheart deals with the bosses in exchange for bribes and other incentives that allow them to maintain their own lavish lifestyles; the government bureaucrats who carry out the orders of their leaders in the banks and corporate boardrooms; and all the other capitalist minions that oversee and help manage capitalist society from their positions of power.

This revolution will abolish class. It will require all who are able to contribute what they can to the work required to satisfy human wants and needs in exchange for free access to the social product. It will replace owners, executives, specialists, one-man management and the like with collective control. It will eliminate the division of labor, allowing each individual to realize their full potential. It will transform education in a natural process of life. It will socialize any undesirable labor that cannot be mechanized and open the way for all to participate in meaningful work.

This revolution will abolish private ownership of the means of production. It will bring the tools and technology under the direct control of those who work them. It will eliminate profit motives and reorient production and research toward meeting human requirements.

This revolution will abolish the capitalist state and government bureaucracy. It will do away with "professional politicians" and their party organizations. It will allow all those who contribute to socially necessary labor to exercise power directly through bodies created for that purpose. When representation is necessary, it will be selected via open voting, permanently accountable, and subject to instant recall.

This revolution will abolish the armed forces of the state. It will train and arm the populace so that it can defend itself if required. Any leadership required for specific tasks or campaigns will be directly elected, fully accountable, and subject to recall at all times. It will not allow for the rise of self-interested military leaders or unaccountable secret police.

This revolution will transform the media into an open avenue available to all of society. It will eliminate the profit motive in news, entertainment and the arts, unleashing the truth and allowing real human creativity to flourish.

In other words, this will be a revolution by the toiling majority against all those classes who, one way or another, live off of the fruits of their labor.

It is this revolution which will pave the way for the creation of a classless, global society in which humanity will finally be able to develop to its full potential, free from the chains of exploitation and oppression. It is this revolution that will lay the foundation for a community fit for human beings. It is this revolution that the workers of the world must unite and fight for.

Notes

1. Karl Marx, *The Civil War in France* (Peking: Foreign Languages Press, 1977), p. 74.

2. Jeremy Brecher, *Strike!* (San Francisco: Straight Arrow Books, 1972), pp. 17-18.

3. Ibid, p. 19

4. BAVARIAN SOVIET IS OUSTED. The New York Times. Sunday, April 13, 1919.

5. Ronald I Kowalski, *The Russian Revolution: 1917-1921 (*London: Routledge, 1997*)*, p. 91.

6. In his *The Civil War in France*, Karl Marx--who, despite being referenced by bureaucrats the world over seeking to justify their actions in the name of "Marxism" contributed greatly to the theory of workers' socialism-- mentioned this as a characteristic of workers' rule when explaining that the first decree of the Paris Commune was "the suppression of the standing army, and the substitution for it of the armed people."

    In his first draft of *The Civil War in France*, Marx wrote: "The whole sham of State mysteries and State pretensions was done away [with] by a Commune, mostly consisting of simple working men, organizing the defence of Paris, carrying war against the praetorians of Bonaparte, securing the approvisionnement of that immense town, filling all the posts hitherto divided between government, police, and prefecture, doing their work publicly, simply, under the most difficult and complicated circumstances, and doing it, as Milton did his Paradise Lost, for a few pounds, acting in bright daylight, with no pretensions to infallibility, not hiding itself behind circumlocution offices, not ashamed to confess blunders by correcting them. Making in one order the public functions – military, administrative, political – real workmen's functions, instead of the hidden attributes of a trained caste... Whatever the merits of the single measures of the Commune, its greatest measure was its own organization, extemporized with the foreign enemy at one door, and the class enemy at the other, proving by its life its vitality, confirming its thesis by its action."

7. John Erickson, *The Soviet high command: A military-political history, 1918-1941* (New York: St Martin's Press, 1962), p. 34.

8. *The Russian Revolution.* Ibid, p. 85.

9. Leon Trotsky, *Sochineniya* (works), Vol. XV, p. 126.

68

10. Leon Trotsky. "The Struggle for Cultured Speech." Pravda, May 15, 1923. http://www.marxists.org/archive/trotsky/women/life/23_05_16.htm

11. R.V. Daniels, The Conscience of the Revolution: Communist Opposition in Soviet Russia (Cambridge, MA: Harvard University Press, 1960), p. 107.

12. The Russian Revolution. Ibid, p. 85.

13. Alexandra Kollontai, "The Workers' Opposition." http://www.marxists.org/archive/kollonta/1921/workers-opposition/index.htm

14. J. Lauritsen and D. Thorstad, The Early Homosexual Rights Movement 1864-1935 (Sebastopol, CA: Times Change Press, 1995).

15. J. Meisel and E. S. Kozera, eds., Materials for the Study of the Soviet System (Ann Arbor: G. Wahr Pub. Co., 1953).

16. The Russian Revolution. Ibid, p. 149.

17. The Russian Revolution. Ibid, p. 149.

18. Cunningham, John. Hungary 1919 - 133 days of workers' rule. http://www.workersliberty.org/node/2322

19. Warren Lerner, A History of Socialism and Communism in Modern Times: Theorists, Activists and Humanists (Englewood Cliffs, NJ: Prentice-Hall, 1982), p. 132.

20. Ibid, p. 203.

21. Bianco Lucien, Origins of the Chinese Revolution, 1915-1949 (Palo Alto, CA: Stanford University Press, 1971), p. 82

22. Ibid, pp. 83-84.

23. John Robottom, China in Revolution: From Sun Yat-sen to Mao Tse-Tung (New York: McGraw-Hill, 1971), p. 112.

24. Charles Hobday, Communist and Marxist Parties of the World (St. Andrews: Cartermill International, 1986), p. 165.

25. Miranda Vickers, The Albanians: a modern history (New York: St. Martin's Press, 10010), p. 181.

26. Ibid, p. 194.

27. http://www.korea-dpr.com/business.htm

28. Pol Pot, Long Live The 17th Anniversary of the Communist Party of Kampuchea (Chicago: Liberator Press, 1978), pp. 18-20.

29. Suzanne Jolicoeur Katsikas, The Arch of Socialist Revolutions,

(Cambridge, MA: Schenkman Publishing Company, 1982), p. 133.

30. Maurice Zeitlin, "Cuba: Revolution without a Blueprint," in Irving Louis Horowitz ed., *Cuban Communism* (New Brunswick, NJ: Transaction Books, 1977), p. 203.

31. Robert Breene Jr., *Latin American Political Yearbook 2000* (Piscataway, NJ: Transaction Publishers, 2001), p. 165.

Time Line

1871 - Creation of Paris Commune marks first real attempt by working class to take power. Commune is short lived.

1877 - Creation of St. Louis Commune marks second significant attempt at control by working class. Second attempt fares no better than first.

1917 - October Revolution takes place in the Russian Empire. The working class takes power and holds onto it for the first time in world history.

1910 - Imperialist Japan annexes Korea.

1919 - Working class reaches for power in Bavaria. Newly formed "Republic of Councils" is drowned in blood soon after.

1919 - Inspired by occurrences in Russia, petty-bourgeois elements make a play for power with the creation of the "Hungarian Soviet Republic."

1920 - State power falls out of the hands of the working class in Russia and associated countries as petty-bourgeois socialists take control.

1921 - White Army is driven from Mongolia by Soviet

forces. Petty-bourgeois socialists seize power with the support of the Kremlin.

1929 - Severe capitalist crisis known as the Great Depression begins.

1936 - As civil war breaks out in Spain, workers in several areas take means of production under their control. Failure to advance the overthrow of capitalism throughout the country would lead to eventual defeat of the nascent emancipatory movement.

1939 - World War II breaks out.

1944 - Soviet Army drives Nazis out of Poland. Petty-bourgeoisie comes to power.

1944 - Soviet Army occupies Romania. Capitalism is overthrown as Petty-bourgeois bureaucrats take control of the country.

1944 - Nazi puppets overthrown in USSR-backed coup in Bulgaria. Petty-bourgeois class rule begins.

1944 - Soviet Army wrests control of Czechoslovakia from Nazis. Petty-bourgeois bureaucrats begin to jockey for power.

1944 - Communist partisans victorious in Albania.

Petty-bourgeoisie seizes power.

1945 - Communist-led partisans drive occupiers from Yugoslavia with the help of Soviet Army. Federal People's Republic of Yugoslavia formed as petty-bourgeoisie takes power.

1945 - Soviet Army occupies Hungary. Capitalism is subsequently overthrown as petty-bourgeoisie bureaucrats loyal to Moscow assume power.

1945 - Soviet Army takes Berlin, paving the way for the eventual ascendency of the petty-bourgeoisie to power in the eastern part of Germany.

1945 - After Japanese surrender, Soviet and U.S. forces each occupy half of Korea.

1946 - People's Republic of Bulgaria officially proclaimed.

1946 - Socialist People's Republic of Albania founded.

1947 - Romania officially becomes a People's Republic.

1948 - Creation of People's Republic of Czechoslovakia announced.

1948 - Creation of new capitalist state in U.S.-occupied half of Korea is followed by expropriations and creation of petty-bourgeois socialist state in the Soviet-occupied northern half.

1949 - German Democratic Republic is officially proclaimed in East Germany.

1949 - Communist-led People's Liberation Army defeats nationalists after years of civil war in China, putting the petty-bourgeoisie in power.

1952 - Poland officially becomes the People's Republic of Poland.

1953 - Strikes break out across East Germany after rulers intensify work. Soviet Army steps in to crush the uprising.

1956 - Working class revolts in Hungary, eventually setting up workers councils and fighting for power.

1959 - Broad national alliance led by petty-bourgeoisie socialists grouped around Fidel Castro overthrows U.S.-backed dictatorship of Fulgencio Batista, paving the way for the seizure of power.

1968 - Massive demonstrations and other actions in France mark high point of international wave of open struggle.

1969 - Petty-bourgeois socialism begins in Somalia as Supreme Revolutionary Council takes control.

1974 - Petty-bourgeois bureaucrats seize power in Ethiopia as military officer group ushers in revolutionary change from above.

1975 - After years of war, Viet Nam is united under the control of the petty-bourgeoisie as the Communist forces take Saigon.

1975 - Petty-bourgeoisie seizes power in Laos as the socialist Lao People's Revolutionary Party overthrows King Savang Vatthana.

1975 - Petty-bourgeois elements take control as Khmer Rouge emerges victorious in Cambodia.

1978 - Vietnamese forces invade Cambodia, overthrowing Khmer Rouge and installing loyal bureaucrats in the process.

1978 - Capitalist-oriented economic reforms enacted in China.

1980 - Major strikes break out in Poland.

1986 - Pro-capitalist "doi moi" policy implemented in Viet Nam.

1986 - Pro-Capitalist "New Economic Mechanism" introduced in Laos.

1989 - Fundamental changes at all levels of society and declaration of "free market orientation" by elements of Vietnamese-sponsored regime in Cambodia mark official reintroduction of capitalism.

1989 - Petty-bourgeois socialism overthrown in Poland. New capitalist state is formed.

1989 - Protests break out in Mongolia and East Germany,

1989 - Petty-bourgeois socialism overturned in Bulgaria.

1989 - After years of stagnation and unrest, petty-bourgeois socialism is brought to a close in Czechoslovakia.

1989 - Protests become widespread in Romania. Petty-bourgeoisie is overthrown as leader Nicolae Ceauşescu and wife are executed on national television.

1989 - Tiananmen Square Massacre is put down in Beijing. Transformations follow as capitalist class takes power in China.

1990 - East Germany is integrated into capitalist Federal Republic of Germany.

1991 – Petty-bourgeois rule ends in Viet Nam as socialist forms are dismantled at Seventh Congress of the Communist Party.

1991 - Petty-bourgeois rule comes to a close in Laos. New constitution marks establishment of capitalist state.

1991 - Overthrow of the Dergue marks the end of bureaucratic rule in Ethiopia.

1991 - Petty-bourgeois socialism dealt death blow in Somalia as bureaucratic regime is overthrown by warlord forces.

1991 - The last remnants of petty-bourgeois socialism crumble away in Albania.

2008 - Global capitalist systems enters deepest crisis since the Great Depression.

2011 – Renewed struggle breaks out in several countries.